CW00937615

Meditation
for
Beginners

The Complete Handbook of Scripts and

Techniques for Everyday Life

by

Craig Coggle

*For all those seeking to be the change
they want to see in the world*

PREFACE

Thank you for picking up Meditation for Beginners, I hope you find great benefit from it. If you've never thought that you could meditate or become a meditator, well congratulations, you've taken your first step.

This guide gives you an outline of some basic meditation techniques that I use, taken from a range of sources. I have laid it out in 10 steps so that you can follow along in your own time scale.

Just remember, meditation is not a race and there's no prize for finishing first.

So, I hope you enjoy this book and the information it brings. I have included a number of meditation scripts that you can either read and follow as you meditate or else recite onto your phone or tablet and listen back to.

Peace.

CONTENTS

BEFORE WE BEGIN

When you decide to start meditating it is easy to fantasize about how many hours you will sit for. You could probably picture yourself dressed in flowing robes, sitting proudly on a wooden terrace and looking out at Tibetan Mountains day after day.

The urge will be to sit for 2 or 3 hours right from the start, or to try a 10-day retreat with no previous experience. The patient approach will be better; you must treat it as a beginner jogger would treat their first attempt at long distance running.

If you were starting jogging, let's say you were planning to run a marathon in a years' time, you would approach very tentatively. First you would buy your shoes and check out the new Lycra gear, get all dressed up. Then you would get your water bottle organized and find the right socks and headwear.

You see… you are showing some trepidation and some respect to the task at hand not diving right in. Only after this process would you venture out, slowly.

A few laps of the park or a couple of times round the block. Then you start to notice your new shoes biting into your heels a bit. The neck of your T-shirt is rubbing against your neck and one side of your headphones keeps falling out. Thank goodness you're not running the marathon yet.

So it is with meditation. It looks easy but it can be hard; really tough. You will have good days and bad days but that's not really the point. When you start to rise to the challenge of meditation, you are becoming attached to 'being a meditator' and that's not meditation.

So before we begin, let's say that meditation is just sitting. It's not an exercise in stamina or physical discipline and it's not something that needs to be done to a punishing schedule. If you make it a punishing schedule then you will just burn out with it and stop.

Don't go searching for answers or some escape from life with meditation; your problems will still be there when you get off the cushion. Having said that, hopefully you will find some inner strength and some clarity from meditation that will let you handle things a little better. Also perhaps, when you least expect it, you will experience the first flowering of bliss in your mind.

This beginner's meditation guide outlines a basic method that I use. You can complete it in the timescale of your choosing; you may prefer to spend one day, a few days, or even a week, on each stage. Take your time and do what feels right.

LETTING GO

This is the first time that you are going to sit; but no big deal. Just sit on your own without TV or radio, without books or conversations or music, without distractions. You are going to sit and just let go of all of that stuff.

There are many opinions on posture and how to sit, so I'll give you a view from my experience. I find trying to meditate in a comfy chair or when lying down really difficult; I think I am conditioned to respond to this by falling asleep or at least getting dozy.

I prefer an upright half lotus position with the spine straight and my head tilted down slightly in front. I use a meditation cushion underneath me with my legs crossed in front, this posture gives me some stability so that I can sit for some time; the straight spine helps to keep me alert. I place a hand on each knee and touch the thumb and first finger of each hand together.

This also helps me achieve a balanced poise. I close me eyes because, for my own preference, it feels more sacred and private to do so.

I sit like this and feel almost like a mountain; centred, strong, poised and erect. Try different ways of sitting for yourself, but aim for balance and a straight spine. Close your eyes, or have them half open if you are having trouble staying awake.

Follow the rhythm of your breath without changing it in any way and start to pay attention to the flow of thoughts through your mind. The mind is like a restless imp and once the distractions are removed the chatter can tend to take over; which it will. So you are going to let the mind chatter and just let go as best you can. Treat it like a circus playing out as you observe.

When you meditate you can let go of your role, of your situation, of your issues. You can let go of your personal histories and just be alone within yourself. Yet you are never really alone, ever... more on that later.

For now, just sit. Don't count breaths or worry about how long it has been, simply sit with you and begin to let go of the need to be anywhere, to be anyone, or to be anything.

Enjoy the luxury of abandoning time whilst you meditate, and just let go of all the baggage that you usually have to carry around with you.

Let go.

Script For Letting Go

Close your eyes and get comfortable as you sit with a straight, relaxed spine.

Become aware of your breathing.

In through the nose and out through the mouth.

Follow the rhythm of your breath without changing it in any way.

Pay attention to the flow of thoughts through your mind.

Let the mind chatter and let go as of any attachment to your thoughts.

Let go of your role.

Let go of your situation.

Let go of your issues.

Let go of your personal history and be alone within yourself.

Just sit.

Simply sit with you and begin to let go of the need to be anywhere, to be anyone, or to be anything.

Enjoy the luxury of abandoning time whilst you meditate.

Let go of all the baggage that you usually have to carry around with you.

Let go.

OBSERVE THE BODY

First you sit.

Arrange yourself comfortably into your posture and then start to become aware of your mind chatter. I talked in the last step about the Burmese posture that I prefer to use but there are plenty of other popular positions; so feel free to use the Burmese technique yourself, or else one that you are comfortable with. Look back at the Step 1 session if you missed it.

As you sit, allow your awareness to take in the mind chatter and then slowly begin to let go of your connection to it; just let it carry on without any attachment. Let go of needing to respond to your mind and allow your breathing to settle into an even rhythm; centre yourself like a mountain.

In this meditation you will begin to observe the body. As you still yourself you will find not only that the mind chatter begins to flare up but also that a whole raft of physical sensations appear. You will feel all kinds of tickles, itches, pains, ticks and twitches; such a commotion just because you are sitting.

Beads of sweat prickling on your skin or a fly landing on your arm… such agony.

The aim in this step is to bring your attention to each of these sensations and to simply observe them. Maybe watch how each one transforms when you place your attention onto it.

An important part of this meditation is to quiet the selective and judgmental mind. This is the one that always has an opinion on things: 'I like that' or 'I don't like that' with a bit of 'Ooh, that really hurts' and 'I'm a bit hot, I'm a bit cold'.

Weighing up, labelling, commenting; it's what you have been trained to do through society, media and education.

You will let go of this during this meditation so that a sensation is simply a sensation, a tickle is a tickle and an itch, well it can be almost unbearable, but it's still just an itch.

Work to maintain your equilibrium and your poise.

Move your attention around the body and become aware of each sensation. Let go of wanting to control or comment.

Breathe.

Script For Observing The Body

First sit comfortably.

Arrange yourself into your posture and become aware of your mind chatter.

Allow your awareness to take in the mind chatter and then slowly begin to let go of your connection to it.

Become aware of the physical sensation of your body.

Allow your awareness to move to wherever you feel the sensation.

Hold your focus there.

Go deeper into that feeling.

Become aware.

Go deeper.

Notice what else arises.

Allow your awareness to move there.

Watch how each sensation transforms when you place your attention onto it.

Allow your mind to settle.

Keep moving your attention around the body and become aware of each sensation.

Let go of wanting to control or comment.

Breathe.

PRESENT MOMENT AWARENESS

Sit in your posture and begin to centre yourself. Straighten your spine and feel the beautiful poise and balance that you are establishing.

Follow your breath for a few moments and begin to become aware of how your body feels today. Focus on a certain part of the body, a certain sensation. Feel the skin warm slightly as you put your attention onto it; move to another area and enjoy the quiet, timeless feeling of letting go.

Become aware of your mind chatter 'circus'; just quietly observe your thoughts without becoming emotionally attached to them.

In the last step you looked at the selective and judgmental mind manifesting itself as we sat and observed the body; this thinking mind is a real obstacle to silent awareness. Now you will work on overcoming this inner commentary.

As you sit, watch each moment as closely as you can as each one appears. Before you get chance to comment or have an opinion, shift awareness to the next moment.

We used to have a TV show in the UK called The Generation Game, which used to end with a conveyor belt challenge. In that example, contestants are trying to give all of their attention to each item on the conveyor belt so that they can remember it later on, and then claim it as a prize. As they look at each prize the next one comes along, then the next. There is no time to even think whether they want to win that one or not because the belt keeps moving.

Focus on each moment as it comes to you on this metaphorical conveyor belt. Don't make notes on the experience because to do so means that you will miss the next moment. When you become perfectly aware of each moment then you will not have time to chatter to yourself, the mind will quiet and become silent awareness.

What a relief to remove this great burden that you have carried with you for so many years, this baggage of mind chatter.

This is something that you can take with you into your everyday life as well, when you are away from the cushion and a part of the day-to-day world. When you feel overwhelmed in a certain situation then just recall your silent moment-to-moment awareness, begin to observe each moment and close down the mind chatter through presence.

Mindful always.

OBSERVE THE BREATH (PART I)

You've spent at least three days (maybe longer), sitting with yourself in meditation. You've become used to a certain posture and have some experience of letting go of your minds' chatter. You have observed the sensations present in the body and started to also become aware of each present moment without judging it or trying to change it in any way.

Now we will be taking this one step further and instead of becoming silently aware of each moment that touches the mind, we will instead use the silent awareness of one thing.

The breath.

This is often the starting point for many meditation programs, but really you need to develop the foundations that we have worked on in previous entries. If you have no skill at letting go of the mind chatter then your awareness of the breath will be very hard to accomplish.

Instead, make sure that you are comfortable letting go of the body sensations and the mind chatter and that you also have begun to experience silent present moment awareness.

Now you can begin to fix your attention on the breath; this

will narrow the diversity of your consciousness (all of those moments) down to one thing. You will follow the breath moment to moment without interruption, just focus on the experience of the breath that is happening now. Because the two obstacles to this have already been worked on (mind circus and inner dialogues) you may find you can do this comfortably. If it is a struggle then spend some more time going over days 1, 2, and 3 until you are comfortable with the techniques.

When you are able, I recommend focusing on the breath at the tip of the nose or just under the nostrils. This is the method taught in the Vipassana tradition and I find it the most effective. You should be able to feel the in and out breath right there at the nostrils, with full awareness.

Experience the breath as you sit, without trying to force it or influence it in any way. If it begins to transform as you sit, if it gets slower for instance, that is okay; simply sit and experience it through each moment. You are an observer and you can let go.

Set your meditation timer.

Breath in. Breath out.

OBSERVE THE BREATH (PART II)

There are many obstacles that appear when you begin to meditate in earnest. Some of the more common ones are: sleepiness, restless mind, pain and discomfort, daydreaming, attachment to thoughts, impatience.

These crop up in some form for just about everyone and can be combatted with awareness of breath:

- Awareness of breath will counter sleepiness, you can always force the breath a little in these early stages to wake yourself up a bit; also try lifting your head up a little.
- Awareness of breath will still the mind, and snap it into focus if it is daydreaming.
- Awareness of breath will revert your mind to the present moment if you find that you have been lost in thought.
- Awareness of breath will help you settle in presence if you are impatiently listening for the timer to be up.
- Awareness of breath will take energy from body sensations.

Meditating by observing the breath is really a lifetime study so I permit myself to repeat the same meditation as Step 4.

Really, you could spend months and years at this stage and still be progressing towards stillness and clarity of mind.

For this step you sit, settle the mind, and gently become aware of each moment that you are experiencing. Then you will bring your attention on to the experience of your breathing by focusing on the tip of your nose, at the nostrils.

You should feel the skin slightly cool on each in breath and perhaps warm a little on each out breath. This may help you focus but don't get wrapped up too much in the sensations but in the breath cycle itself. Draw yourself into this rhythm and the experience of breathing.

Finally, I suggest that you put a time limit on this meditation - perhaps 5 or 10 minutes. Set a timer for your chosen period and begin to meditate. When the timer rings, slowly bring yourself back to the room, open your eyes and take a deep breath ready to continue with your day.

Calm.

PRESENT MOMENT AWARENESS OF BREATH

When meditation happens with very little effort, you will experience true peace and balance with pure clarity of mind. By dealing with the distractions and obstacles to meditation as you have in the previous steps you are setting the ground for something quite special to occur.

When you work on removing hindrances you allow the meditation to bloom unaided, almost by itself. Think of your work as blowing away dark clouds to leave a tranquil blue sky; that sky was always there but up to now had been obscured.

Clouds obscure your silent mind and your work is to clear them through focus and awareness.

Now we extend your observation of the breath so that you experience every present moment of each breath. As you sit and centre yourself begin to touch the origin of the in-breath, the first sensation of breath arising. Feel the whole of the next in-breath cycle, every moment. When the in-breath finishes you will feel a pause, a short suspension until eventually the out-breath begins.

Feel every sensation of the out-breath back to a pause before the next in-breath and the cycle repeating again.

Open up your awareness from the tip of the nose to include everywhere that you experience the breath: the abdomen; your chest; your shoulders; your inner self.

You can't force this process or struggle with it, just continue to let go of everything that you are and allow it to be. It is always there, waiting to reveal itself.

Continue to observe the breath cycles over and over as long as it is comfortable to do so, you are allowing the mind to automatically settle into full present moment awareness.

Refrain from commenting: 'I'm doing it! I'm doing it!', you can always reflect on this later after you have finished your practice. Any comments at this stage will cause the silent mind to retreat and the ego to come charging in with its neediness.

By now you are probably meditating for 10 minutes at a time and you can gradually increase for as long as you feel comfortable holding your awareness on the full breath cycle. I don't personally meditate for hours on end but there is certainly a shift in depth of stillness when you move past 30 minutes or so.

This will be different for each of you but I would expect you to achieve great results by meditating from between 30 - 40 minutes at a time.

Observe the breath fully.

Be present fully.

Script For Observing The Breath

Sit, settle the mind, and gently become aware of each moment that you are experiencing.

Observe your breathing.

Notice how your breath flows in and out.

Make no effort to change your breathing in any way, simply notice how your body breathes.

Your body knows how much air it needs.

Sit quietly and visualize your breath flowing gently in and out of your body.

When your attention wanders, as it will, just focus back again on your breathing.

Don't dwell on any stray thoughts, simply let them pass.

See how your breath continues to flow and feel the sensations at the entrance to your nostrils.

Breathe deeply.

Calmly.

Notice the stages of a complete breath... from the in breath... to the pause that follows... the exhale... and the pause before taking another breath.

Become aware of the slight pauses between each breath.

Feel the air entering at the nostrils.

Imagine the air inside your body after you inhale, filling your body gently.

Feel your chest and stomach gently rise and fall with each breath.

See how calm and gentle your breathing is, and how relaxed your body feels.

Breathe.

When you are ready... gently reawaken your body and mind.

Keeping your eyes closed, notice the sounds around you.

Feel the floor beneath you.

Feel your clothes against your body.

Wiggle your fingers and toes.

Shrug your shoulders.

Open your eyes, and remain sitting for a few moments longer.

Straighten out your legs, and stretch your arms and legs gently.

Sit for a few moments more, enjoying how relaxed you feel, and experiencing your body reawaken and your mind returning to its usual level of alertness.

BODY SCAN

Up to this point you have developed a strong foundation in breath and present moment awareness; now you can extend this meditation to include the physical body.

Sit in your posture and allow your mind to settle. Observe the breath for a while and bring your full attention to the present moment. Continue to focus on the breath until you are fully present, remember to let go of your opinions and mind chatter as you do this.

Now bring your attention to the top of your head, the crown. Become aware of any sensations that are there and bring your awareness to them. Simply let them be and observe.

You are going to be scanning the whole body with this focused attention, slowly and with intention.

From the crown of your head bring your attention down your face from the forehead to the eyes, nose, lips, cheeks, chin. Continue to move downwards to the neck, the shoulders, chest, arms, wrists, and hands. You are allowing the experience of all the sensations that you find to come into your full awareness.

Continue down from your chest to the torso, stomach,

waist, groin, your thighs, knees, down to your feet and toes.

Return the scan slowly back to the crown of your head, all the time deliberately observing as you go. Now repeat this body scan but begin to move beneath the surface of the skin. To me this feels like a 3D sweep through the body rather than the 2D surface scan.

Experience the muscle structure under the skin, feel your skeleton, keep scanning to include your organs, nervous system, blood vessels. You can take your time with this, just allow the experience to be and let go of any meaning.

Keep systematically scanning through your entire body from crown to toes and back again.
When your timer sounds bring yourself back into the room and give thanks for your meditation.

Grateful.

Script For Body Scan

Sit in your posture and allow your mind to settle.

Observe the breath for a while and bring your full attention to the present moment.

Continue to focus on the breath until you are fully present, remember to let go of your opinions and mind chatter as you do this.

Bring your attention to the top of your head, the crown.

Become aware of any sensations that are there and bring your awareness to them. Simply let them be and observe.

From the crown of your head bring your attention down your face from the forehead to the eyes.

Nose.

Lips.

Cheeks.

Chin.

Continue to move downwards to the neck, the shoulders, chest, arms, wrists, and hands.

Allow the experience of all the sensations that you find to come into your full awareness.

Continue down from your chest to the torso.

Stomach.

Waist.

Groin.

Thighs.

Knees, and down to your feet and toes.

Now slowly return the scan back to the crown of your head, all the time deliberately observing as you go.

Now repeat this body scan but begin to move beneath the surface of the skin.

Experience the muscle structure under the skin.

Feel your skeleton.

Continue scanning to include your organs, nervous system, blood vessels.

Slowly move from each part of your internal body and allow the experience to deepen.

Keep systematically scanning through your entire body from crown to toes and back again.

When your timer sounds bring yourself back into the room and give thanks for your meditation.

ENERGY ARISING

I wanted to share this meditation technique with you for Step 8. It's something that I discovered myself but have since come across it being used as a technique by others; perhaps you might have experienced something similar to the techniques of Kundalini, active meditations, or yoga.

I found that after I'd worked with the body scan for a while I began to experience a spreading of awareness over a larger area of the body. I don't want you to think that the experience that I describe is in anyway the right one, or indeed exactly what you will feel, but you may get something similar to this.

As the awareness opens out I focus on the lower half of my body. I feel a warmth throughout my legs, a tingling through the flesh.

I used to think that this was just my legs falling asleep or getting pins and needles but after the meditation I always found that there was no pain or discomfort in my legs at all; often they felt more refreshed than usual.

The more I focus on this feeling the more this energy expands; now I start to imagine this energy as a soft white light surrounding my legs. I sit with this energy for a while and enjoy its power before allowing it to move up through the spine towards the crown of my head.

From here the energy expands until I am sitting fully bathed in this feeling of resurgence and vitality.

This is a very refreshing and uplifting meditation to try, one that combines the bliss of silently letting go with the restoring energy of a workout.

You can sit with this energy for as long as you can keep it in your presence, or else set a timer and stay with this feeling until the end of your session.

Try this process a few times over the next few days and each time allow this energy to expand within your body and move up and down your spine, let it clear blockages and open up the energy channels within you.

Follow its energy.

Bliss.

DEEP CONTENTMENT

Once you have established a foundation of regular effective practice you will probably find settling into full awareness of breath and body becomes an essential part of your day.

I suppose its not wise to become attached to meditation, in the same way as anything else, but sometimes I feel a bit unbalanced until I've had my chance to sit and do my practice.

Having said that, you will still have times when the meditation drags, when the mind won't settle and when anxiety and doubt about creeps in. This is normal and the good news is that this will get less and less the more established your practice becomes.

You will also find your meditations becoming deeper at this stage, leading you to experience a full and deep contentment within mind.

Sit in your posture and allow the mind to settle.

Bring yourself to the present moment and begin to observe and experience your breath.

Follow the breath with your focus, after some time you

will find that the breath starts to lose its distinct in and out points of reference - it is what Ajahn Brahm calls the 'beautiful breath'.

The breath calms down and becomes smoother; often you can't discern the breath at all or you may experience the feeling of it slowing down.

This is the point that the mind experiences deep contentment, so allow it to come as you just sit with your calm and effortless breath. It is useful to remember that this state exists naturally within us and it reveals itself to us once we remove the obstacles of mind chatter and scattered focused.

Remember as well that you don't have to do anything at this stage; any kind of effort will often burst the bubble and cause the bliss to disperse.

You have to abandon yourself to this process, let go of having to direct it or make it happen. Have a break from effort and trying, just be with the experience.

Allow the breath to disappear, allow contentment to envelop the mind.

Sit in stillness and let go of ego.

Still.

LETTING GO REPRISE

I'm not going to pretend that on Step 10 we've suddenly reached enlightenment and I'm sure you got the message by now that this is really just an arbitrary way for me to lay out the information. In reality each stage could take months, if not years, of dedicated practice.

I don't think enlightenment needs to be some sort of goal here. Sitting everyday in silent awareness of the present moment will make such a difference to your balance in life.

Practicing following your breath, experiencing the body sensations in the moment, and generating your own revitalizing energy will bring a deep and lasting peace and contentment to your everyday outlook. Keep sitting regularly; make it your own personal project, your gift to yourself.

After sometime practicing you will find that you are mindful more during the day, you will be less quick to criticize and take offense with what others say.

A personal equanimity will help you handle the difficult dynamics of life and not just feel that you are reacting to a series of uncontrollable events. I guess that's why I value meditation and that feeling of balance and perspective that it brings.

So far we have:
- Calmed our mind chatter.
- Become aware of the present moment.
- Used awareness of the breath as a meditation technique.
- Explored the sensations of the body.
- Developed full awareness of the breath in the moment.
- Experienced energy arising in the body.
- Allowed contentment to emerge through the disappearing breath.

As a final thought I wanted to mention how the disappearing breath eventually expands to become the experience of the dissolving of the body.

As you are sitting, observing your breath and scanning your body you will reach a stage where the physical form begins to disappear. Just for a moment you will feel no boundary between yourself and the rest of the universe.

There is no separation; there is no body.

There is just awareness.

You will find this to be quite a fleeting experience at first, but it will gradually stay with you longer and longer allowing you to feel a connection to everything that is. Again, don't try to make it happen but allow it to happen through letting go.

What you are doing is releasing your physical identity,

your ego. When you experience that you are part of the infinite universe, things that seem so urgent or serious in your life are placed into a different perspective.

This feeling of unity can comfort you and inspire you.

Sit and let the body dissolve.

Feel the connection to the infinite universe and let go of the small ego.

Let go.

Let go.

Let go.

APPENDIX

SCRIPT FOR LETTING GO

Close your eyes and get comfortable as you sit with a straight, relaxed spine.

Become aware of your breathing.

In through the nose and out through the mouth.

Follow the rhythm of your breath without changing it in any way.

Pay attention to the flow of thoughts through your mind.

Let the mind chatter and let go as of any attachment to your thoughts.

Let go of your role.

Let go of your situation.

Let go of your issues.

Let go of your personal history and be alone within yourself.

Just sit.

Simply sit with you and begin to let go of the need to be anywhere, to be anyone, or to be anything.

Enjoy the luxury of abandoning time whilst you meditate.

Let go of all the baggage that you usually have to carry around with you.

Let go.

SCRIPT FOR OBSERVING THE BODY

First sit comfortably.

Arrange yourself into your posture and become aware of your mind chatter.

Allow your awareness to take in the mind chatter and then slowly begin to let go of your connection to it.

Become aware of the physical sensation of your body.

Allow your awareness to move to wherever you feel the sensation.

Hold your focus there.

Go deeper into that feeling.

Become aware.

Go deeper.

Notice what else arises.

Allow your awareness to move there.

Watch how each sensation transforms when you place your attention onto it.

Allow your mind to settle.

Keep moving your attention around the body and become aware of each sensation.

Let go of wanting to control or comment.

Breathe.

SCRIPT FOR OBSERVING THE BREATH

Sit, settle the mind, and gently become aware of each moment that you are experiencing.

Observe your breathing.

Notice how your breath flows in and out.

Make no effort to change your breathing in any way, simply notice how your body breathes.

Your body knows how much air it needs.

Sit quietly and visualize your breath flowing gently in and out of your body.

When your attention wanders, as it will, just focus back again on your breathing.

Don't dwell on any stray thoughts simply let them pass.

See how your breath continues to flow and feel the sensations at the entrance to your nostrils.

Breathe deeply.

Calmly.

Notice the stages of a complete breath... from the in breath... to the pause that follows... the exhale... and the pause before taking another breath.

Become aware of the slight pauses between each breath.

Feel the air entering at the nostrils.

Imagine the air inside your body after you inhale, filling your body gently.

Feel your chest and stomach gently rise and fall with each

breath.

See how calm and gentle your breathing is, and how relaxed your body feels.

Breathe.

Breathe.

When you are ready... gently reawaken your body and mind.

Keeping your eyes closed, notice the sounds around you.

Feel the floor beneath you.

Feel your clothes against your body.

Wiggle your fingers and toes.

Shrug your shoulders.

Open your eyes, and remain sitting for a few moments longer.

Straighten out your legs, and stretch your arms and legs gently.

Sit for a few moments more, enjoying how relaxed you feel, and experiencing your body reawaken and your mind returning to its usual level of alertness.

SCRIPT FOR BODY SCAN

Sit in your posture and allow your mind to settle.

Observe the breath for a while and bring your full attention to the present moment.

Continue to focus on the breath until you are fully present, remember to let go of your opinions and mind chatter as you do this.

Bring your attention to the top of your head, the crown.

Become aware of any sensations that are there and bring your awareness to them. Simply let them be and observe.

From the crown of your head bring your attention down your face from the forehead to the eyes.

Nose.

Lips.

Cheeks.

Chin.

Continue to move downwards to the neck, the shoulders, chest, arms, wrists, and hands.

Allow the experience of all the sensations that you find to come into your full awareness.

Continue down from your chest to the torso.

Stomach.

Waist.

Groin.

Thighs.

Knees and down to your feet and toes.

Now slowly return the scan back to the crown of your head, all the time deliberately observing as you go.

Now repeat this body scan but begin to move beneath the surface of the skin.

Experience the muscle structure under the skin.

Feel your skeleton.

Continue scanning to include your organs, nervous system, blood vessels.

Slowly move from each part of your internal body and allow the experience to deepen.

Keep systematically scanning through your entire body from crown to toes and back again.

When your timer sounds bring yourself back into the room and give thanks for your meditation.

ABOUT THE AUTHOR

Craig Coggle lives with his wife and son in North London. He works as an educator and consultant and has published works in Pick The Brain, Tiny Buddha, and Change This.

He is a firm believer in the power and possibility of self-actualization – for each of us to fulfil our potential and find out who we really are, given the right environment.

Craig started meditating over ten years ago and has continued to study the works of many of the meditation masters that have walked this path before: Osho, Charlotte Joko Beck, Jon Kabat-Zinn, Alan Watts, S. N. Goenka, Geshe Kelsang Gyatso, and Daisaku Ikeda.

He continues to write and teach in the hope that the practice of meditation will appear, not as something esoteric and mysterious, but instead as an essential and useful tool that can be of benefit to everyone, every day.

Meet Craig, and discover more resources on meditation and mindfulness, at 21stcenturymonk.net.

Printed in Great Britain
by Amazon

57987007R00030